We hope this book has been informative and helpful on your journey to understanding and celebrating older adults. Thank you for your interest and support!

Title: Grammar in Context

Subtitle: Applying English Grammar in Real-World Situations

Series: The Grammar Bible: Mastering the Rules and Conventions of English

By P. C. Dictionaire

"The English language is the sea which receives tributaries from every region under heaven."
Henry David Thoreau

"The English language is like a broad river on whose bank a few graceful trees are reflected, it is the language of a people who have a great past and who will have a great future."
Joseph Conrad

"The English language is the key to the world."
Neil Gaiman

"The English language is nobody's special property. It is the property of the imagination: it is the property of the language itself."
Derek Walcott

"The English language is the most important language in the world. It's the language of international business, politics, and entertainment."
Richard Branson

"The English language is a river that moves, and sometimes it flows backwards."
Alice Oswald

"The English language is a work in progress. Have fun with it."
Jonathan Culver

Table of Contents

Introduction

The Importance of Context in English Grammar

Effective communication in English requires more than just a mastery of grammar rules and vocabulary. In order to communicate effectively, it is also essential to understand the context in which you are communicating. The context can include the audience, purpose, tone, and cultural norms that shape communication. In this chapter, we will explore the importance of context in English grammar and how it affects communication in different situations.

The Importance of Context in English Grammar:

English grammar is not a set of rigid rules that apply in all situations. Rather, grammar rules are flexible and adaptable to the context in which they are used. For example, the use of contractions, informal language, and slang may be acceptable in casual conversations with friends but not in formal business communication. Similarly, the use of complex sentence structures and technical vocabulary may be appropriate in academic writing but not in everyday conversation.

The context of communication also affects the tone and register of language. Tone refers to the attitude or emotion conveyed in language, while register refers to the level of formality or informality of language. For example, the tone and register of language used in a business meeting will be different from that used in a social gathering.

Understanding the context of communication is essential for effective communication in English. When you understand the context, you are able to use appropriate grammar, vocabulary, tone, and register to convey your message effectively. This can help you avoid misunderstandings, miscommunications, and unintended consequences of your words.

Context can also help you interpret the meaning of language. For example, the same words may have different meanings depending on the context in which they are used. The word "cool" may mean "cold" when used to describe the weather, but it may also mean "fashionable" or "impressive" when used to describe a person or an object. Understanding the context can help you interpret the intended meaning of language correctly.

In addition to the linguistic context, cultural context is also important in English grammar. Cultural norms and values shape the way language is used in different cultures. For example, the use of direct language and criticism may be more acceptable in some cultures than in others. Similarly, the use of humor and sarcasm may be more prevalent in some cultures than in others. Understanding the cultural context can help you avoid cultural misunderstandings and communicate effectively across cultures.

Conclusion:

In conclusion, context plays a crucial role in English grammar and effective communication. Understanding the context of communication is essential for using appropriate grammar, vocabulary, tone, and register. It can also help you interpret the meaning of language correctly and avoid cultural misunderstandings. In the following chapters, we will explore the application of English grammar in different real-world situations and how context affects communication in each situation.

Common Grammar Mistakes in Real-World Situations

Grammar is an essential component of effective communication in English. However, even the most proficient English speakers can make grammar mistakes in real-world situations. These mistakes can undermine the clarity and effectiveness of your communication, leading to misunderstandings and misinterpretations. In this chapter, we will explore some common grammar mistakes that occur in real-world situations and how to avoid them.

Common Grammar Mistakes in Real-World Situations:

1. Subject-verb agreement: One common grammar mistake is a lack of agreement between the subject and the verb. This mistake occurs when the verb does not match the number or person of the subject. For example, "The team are playing" instead of "The team is playing" is an example of subject-verb agreement error. To avoid this mistake, always ensure that the verb agrees with the subject in number and person.

2. Pronoun-antecedent agreement: Another common mistake is a lack of agreement between a pronoun and its antecedent. This mistake occurs when the pronoun does not match the gender, number, or person of its antecedent. For

example, "Each student should bring their book" instead of "Each student should bring his or her book" is an example of a pronoun-antecedent agreement error. To avoid this mistake, always ensure that the pronoun agrees with its antecedent in gender, number, and person.

3. Misuse of apostrophes: Apostrophes are often misused in real-world situations, leading to confusion and ambiguity. One common mistake is using apostrophes to indicate plural instead of possessive. For example, "The teacher's give a lot of homework" instead of "The teachers give a lot of homework" is an example of apostrophe misuse. To avoid this mistake, use apostrophes only to indicate possession, not plural.

4. Misuse of commas: Commas are essential for indicating pauses and separating clauses in English. However, they are often misused in real-world situations, leading to run-on sentences and confusion. One common mistake is using too many commas or not using them where they are needed. For example, "She went to the store, and bought milk, bread, and eggs" instead of "She went to the store and bought milk, bread, and eggs" is an example of comma misuse. To avoid this mistake, use commas only where they are needed to indicate pauses or separate clauses.

5. Confusing homophones: Homophones are words that sound the same but have different meanings and spellings. They are often confused in real-world situations, leading to confusion and ambiguity. One common mistake is confusing "their," "there," and "they're." For example, "Their going to the park over there" instead of "They're going to the park over there" is an example of homophone confusion. To avoid this mistake, ensure that you understand the meaning and spelling of each homophone and use it correctly.

Conclusion:

In conclusion, common grammar mistakes can undermine the clarity and effectiveness of your communication in real-world situations. To avoid these mistakes, it is essential to understand the grammar rules and use them correctly. In the following chapters, we will explore practical applications of English grammar in various real-world situations and how to use grammar effectively in each situation.

How This Book Can Help You Improve Your English Language Skills

English is a language that is spoken and written all over the world. It is the primary language of communication in many fields such as business, academia, and entertainment. As such, being proficient in English is a valuable skill that can open doors to new opportunities and enhance one's personal and professional life.

However, mastering English grammar can be a challenging task, even for those who use the language on a daily basis. With so many rules and exceptions to remember, it's easy to make mistakes that can affect the clarity and effectiveness of one's communication.

That's where this book comes in. Grammar in Context: Applying English Grammar in Real-World Situations is designed to help readers improve their English language skills by providing practical guidance and exercises for using grammar effectively in a variety of real-world situations.

Whether you're a student looking to improve your academic writing, a professional seeking to communicate more effectively in the workplace, or simply someone who wants to speak and write English with greater fluency, this book has something to offer.

Through a series of chapters focused on specific types of communication, Grammar in Context provides readers with clear explanations of grammar rules and guidelines, along with examples and exercises that illustrate how to apply these rules in different contexts.

The book also addresses common grammar mistakes and offers tips for avoiding them, helping readers to improve their accuracy and clarity in English communication.

Overall, this book is a valuable resource for anyone who wants to improve their English language skills and communicate more effectively in real-world situations. Whether you're a beginner or an advanced English speaker, Grammar in Context can help you to achieve your goals and enhance your language proficiency.

Chapter 1: Writing Effective Emails
Understanding the Purpose and Audience of Your Email

Writing effective emails is a critical skill in today's digital age. With so much communication happening via email, it's important to be able to craft messages that are clear, concise, and relevant to the recipient.

One of the keys to writing effective emails is understanding the purpose and audience of your message. Before you begin composing your email, take some time to consider what you want to achieve and who your intended audience is.

The purpose of your email may vary depending on the situation. For example, you may be sending an email to a colleague to request information or to a potential employer to inquire about job opportunities. Whatever the purpose of your email, it's important to be clear and concise in your message.

When thinking about your audience, consider their knowledge and experience in the topic you're writing about. For example, if you're writing to a supervisor or a client, they may be more familiar with technical jargon and industry-specific terms. On the other hand, if you're writing to a colleague or a friend, you may need to use simpler language and avoid technical jargon.

Once you have a clear understanding of your purpose and audience, you can start composing your email. Begin by crafting a clear and concise subject line that summarizes the main point of your email. This will help your recipient to quickly understand what your email is about and prioritize it among other messages in their inbox.

When writing the body of your email, keep in mind the purpose and audience of your message. Be sure to provide any necessary background information or context to help your recipient understand the reason for your email. Use clear and simple language, and avoid using jargon or technical terms that your audience may not be familiar with.

When closing your email, be sure to include a clear call to action. This could be a request for information or action, or simply a statement of gratitude for their time and attention.

By taking the time to understand the purpose and audience of your email, you can improve the effectiveness of your communication and increase the likelihood of achieving your intended outcomes.

The Importance of Clear and Concise Language

In today's fast-paced digital world, email has become the primary mode of communication for both personal and professional purposes. Whether you are communicating with colleagues, clients, or customers, it is essential to be able to convey your message clearly and concisely to avoid any misinterpretation or confusion. This is where the importance of clear and concise language comes into play.

Clear and concise language refers to the use of words and phrases that are easy to understand and convey the intended message effectively. When writing an email, it is crucial to keep in mind that the recipient is most likely a busy person who has many other emails to read and respond to. Therefore, your message must be brief and to the point, while still providing all the necessary information.

One of the primary reasons why clear and concise language is so important in email communication is that it helps to avoid misunderstandings. When you are communicating with someone through email, you do not have the benefit of nonverbal cues such as facial expressions and body language to help convey your message. This means that the words you choose must do all the heavy lifting in terms of communicating your thoughts and feelings. By using clear and concise language, you can ensure that your message is understood correctly and that there is no room for misinterpretation.

Another reason why clear and concise language is essential in email communication is that it helps to save time. When you write a long, rambling email that is difficult to understand, the recipient may need to spend additional time trying to decipher your message. This can lead to frustration and a loss of productivity, both for the recipient and for you. By using clear and concise language, you can communicate your message quickly and efficiently, allowing both parties to get on with their work.

Furthermore, clear and concise language also demonstrates professionalism and respect. When you take the time to craft a well-written email that is easy to understand, you show the recipient that you value their time and that you are serious about your communication. This can help to build trust and respect, which can be essential in building and maintaining professional relationships.

In conclusion, clear and concise language is crucial when it comes to writing effective emails. It helps to avoid misunderstandings, saves time, and demonstrates professionalism and respect. When writing an email, take the time to carefully choose your words and phrases, and ensure that your message is easy to understand and conveys your intended meaning.

When it comes to writing effective emails, proper grammar and punctuation are essential. They can help to convey your message clearly and professionally and can prevent any misunderstandings or misinterpretations. Here are some key tips to keep in mind:

1. Use correct spelling: Spelling mistakes can make your email appear unprofessional and careless. Always run a spell-check before sending your email and proofread it carefully to catch any errors that may have been missed.

2. Use proper punctuation: Punctuation can help to clarify your message and make it easier to understand. Use commas, periods, and other punctuation marks where necessary to separate thoughts and ideas and to create a smooth flow of information.

3. Watch your capitalization: Avoid using all caps in your emails, as it can come across as shouting and may be seen as unprofessional. Instead, use capitalization where appropriate, such as for the beginning of sentences, proper nouns, and titles.

4. Use appropriate verb tenses: Make sure to use the correct verb tense when writing your emails. For example, use the present tense when referring to things that are

currently happening and the past tense when referring to things that have already happened.

5. Avoid using slang and abbreviations: While slang and abbreviations may be appropriate in some casual situations, they should generally be avoided in professional emails. Stick to standard English and avoid any potentially confusing or unprofessional language.

6. Use active voice: Writing in the active voice can help to make your message more clear and direct. Use active verbs and avoid passive constructions to create a more engaging and effective email.

7. Be consistent: Consistency is key when it comes to proper grammar and punctuation. Make sure to use the same formatting and punctuation throughout your email to maintain a professional and polished appearance.

By following these tips and taking the time to proofread and edit your emails carefully, you can ensure that your messages are clear, concise, and professional. Proper grammar and punctuation can go a long way in helping you to communicate effectively and build strong professional relationships.

Common Mistakes to Avoid in Email Communication

In the fast-paced world of modern communication, emails have become a ubiquitous mode of communication in the workplace. As emails are often the first point of contact between professionals, it's essential to ensure that they are written effectively and without errors. In this chapter, we will discuss some common mistakes that people make while writing emails and how to avoid them.

1. Using unclear subject lines The subject line is the first thing that the recipient sees when they receive an email. It should be clear, concise, and accurately reflect the content of the email. Avoid using vague subject lines such as "hello" or "urgent" as they do not provide any information to the recipient.

2. Failing to address the recipient properly It's essential to address the recipient of the email appropriately. Use formal titles such as "Mr." or "Ms." if you are writing to someone you don't know well. If you are writing to someone you know well, you can use their first name. Make sure that you spell their name correctly.

3. Writing excessively long emails People have limited attention spans, so it's essential to keep your email concise and to the point. Avoid writing excessively long emails that

are difficult to read and comprehend. Instead, break up your email into smaller, easily digestible chunks.

4. Using inappropriate language It's essential to use appropriate language when writing emails. Avoid using slang or informal language, as it can make you come across as unprofessional. Make sure that you proofread your email carefully for spelling and grammar errors.

5. Not proofreading emails One of the most common mistakes that people make while writing emails is failing to proofread them. It's essential to read your email carefully before sending it to ensure that there are no errors in spelling, grammar, or punctuation. Failing to do so can make you come across as careless and unprofessional.

6. Not responding to emails promptly When you receive an email, it's essential to respond to it promptly, even if it's just to acknowledge receipt of the email. Failing to respond to emails promptly can make you come across as uninterested or unprofessional.

7. Failing to attach files or documents If you have promised to attach a file or document, make sure that you do so before sending the email. Failing to do so can cause delays and inconvenience to the recipient.

In conclusion, writing effective emails is a critical skill for professionals in today's world. By avoiding these common mistakes, you can ensure that your emails are clear, concise, and professional. Remember to proofread your emails carefully, respond promptly, and use appropriate language and you will be well on your way to mastering the art of email communication.

Chapter 2: Giving Presentations
Organizing Your Thoughts and Ideas for Maximum Impact

Organizing your thoughts and ideas is a crucial step in preparing a presentation that will have maximum impact on your audience. In this chapter, we will discuss some strategies for organizing your presentation effectively.

1. Identify your main message Before you begin preparing your presentation, you need to have a clear idea of what you want to say. Identify your main message or key takeaway, and make sure that all your content supports this message.

2. Know your audience Knowing your audience is important because it helps you tailor your message to their needs and interests. Consider factors such as their age, education level, and professional background when planning your presentation.

3. Use an outline An outline is a helpful tool for organizing your thoughts and ideas. Start by creating a rough outline of the main points you want to cover, and then flesh out each point with supporting details.

4. Use a logical structure Your presentation should have a logical structure that is easy for your audience to follow. Begin with an introduction that captures their

attention and provides an overview of your topic. Then, move into the main body of your presentation, where you present your main message and supporting evidence. Finally, end with a conclusion that summarizes your main points and leaves a lasting impression on your audience.

5. Use visual aids Visual aids such as charts, graphs, and images can help reinforce your message and make your presentation more engaging. Use visual aids sparingly, and make sure they are relevant to your message.

6. Practice, practice, practice Once you have organized your thoughts and ideas, it is important to practice your presentation several times. This will help you feel more comfortable and confident, and it will ensure that your delivery is smooth and polished.

In conclusion, organizing your thoughts and ideas is a critical step in preparing a successful presentation. By identifying your main message, knowing your audience, using an outline, using a logical structure, using visual aids, and practicing your delivery, you can ensure that your presentation has maximum impact on your audience.

Using Effective Language and Vocabulary in Your Presentation

When giving a presentation, it's important to use language and vocabulary that effectively conveys your message to your audience. Here are some tips for using effective language and vocabulary in your presentation:

1. Know your audience: Before you start preparing your presentation, it's important to understand your audience. This will help you choose the appropriate language and vocabulary to use. Consider their age, background, education, and familiarity with the topic.

2. Use clear and concise language: Your language should be clear and concise, avoiding jargon, slang, or overly technical terms that may confuse your audience. Use short sentences and simple words to convey your message effectively.

3. Use active voice: Using the active voice makes your presentation more engaging and persuasive. It also helps to simplify complex ideas, making them easier to understand. For example, instead of saying "the report was written by me," say "I wrote the report."

4. Use vivid and descriptive words: Using vivid and descriptive words can help to capture your audience's attention and make your presentation more memorable. For

example, instead of saying "the project was successful," say "the project exceeded our expectations."

5. Use transitional words and phrases: Transitional words and phrases can help to connect ideas and make your presentation flow more smoothly. For example, use words like "however," "therefore," or "in conclusion" to signal a shift in your presentation.

6. Use rhetorical devices: Rhetorical devices are techniques used to create a powerful impact on your audience. These include things like repetition, metaphors, and analogies. For example, you could use a metaphor to explain a complex idea, making it more understandable and relatable.

7. Practice, practice, practice: Finally, practicing your presentation will help you to refine your language and vocabulary. Practice in front of a mirror, record yourself, or present to a friend or family member to get feedback and improve your delivery.

By following these tips, you can use effective language and vocabulary in your presentation to engage and inform your audience, and make your message more memorable.

Using Visual Aids to Enhance Your Message

Visual aids such as slides, images, and videos can be powerful tools to enhance your presentation and help your audience better understand your message. However, it is important to use visual aids effectively and appropriately, as they can also distract or confuse your audience if not used properly. In this section, we will discuss the best practices for using visual aids to enhance your message in presentations.

1. Choose relevant visual aids

When selecting visual aids for your presentation, it is important to choose ones that are relevant and support your message. Consider what information or data can be better communicated visually and choose visual aids that are appropriate for your audience and the purpose of your presentation. Visual aids should not be used just for the sake of using them; they should have a clear purpose and add value to your presentation.

2. Keep it simple

Your visual aids should be easy to understand and not overwhelm your audience with too much information or clutter. Avoid using too many colors, fonts, or graphics that can distract from your message. Use simple and clear visuals that support your message and are easy to read and understand.

3. Use high-quality visuals

The quality of your visual aids can greatly impact their effectiveness. Ensure that your visuals are of high quality and resolution, so that they can be easily seen and read by your audience. Use appropriate images and graphics that are professional and relevant to your message.

4. Practice with your visuals

Before your presentation, practice using your visuals and ensure that they work properly and effectively. Test the sound and video quality of any videos or audio clips you plan to use, and make sure that any slides or graphics are easy to navigate and understand. Familiarize yourself with the flow of your presentation and how your visual aids fit into it.

5. Use visual aids to support your message, not replace it

Visual aids should be used to enhance your message and support what you are saying, not replace it. Avoid relying solely on your visual aids to communicate your message, as this can lead to a lack of engagement with your audience. Use your visuals to supplement your message and provide visual examples or data that support your points.

In summary, using visual aids can greatly enhance your message in presentations if used effectively and appropriately. Choose relevant, simple, and high-quality visuals that support your message, practice using them before your presentation, and use them to supplement your message rather than replace it.

Delivering Your Presentation with Confidence and Clarity

No matter how well you have prepared and how effective your language and visual aids are, if you can't deliver your presentation with confidence and clarity, you may not be able to achieve your objectives. Here are some tips for delivering your presentation with confidence and clarity:

1. Practice, practice, practice: Practice your presentation several times before the actual event. This will help you to be familiar with the content and structure of your presentation, and also to be comfortable with the pacing and timing.

2. Know your audience: Understand the needs and interests of your audience, and tailor your presentation accordingly. Speak in a language that they can understand and relate to.

3. Use body language: Use appropriate body language to support your message. Make eye contact with your audience, use gestures and movements to emphasize key points, and maintain good posture and poise.

4. Speak clearly and audibly: Speak slowly, clearly, and audibly so that your audience can hear and understand you. Avoid speaking too fast, or too softly.

5. Use vocal variety: Use variations in pitch, tone, and speed to add interest and emphasis to your message. Avoid speaking in a monotone or robotic voice.

6. Be natural and authentic: Be yourself, and speak in a natural and authentic way. Avoid trying to be someone you are not, or using language that is not natural to you.

7. Manage nervousness: It is natural to feel nervous before a presentation, but try to manage your nervousness so that it does not affect your performance. Take deep breaths, visualize success, and focus on your message and audience.

By following these tips, you can deliver your presentation with confidence and clarity, and engage your audience effectively. Remember, your objective is to communicate your message in the most effective way possible, and to achieve your desired outcomes.

Chapter 3: Writing Reports and Proposals
Understanding the Structure and Purpose of Reports and Proposals

Writing reports and proposals is an essential aspect of business communication. Whether you are writing a report to present research findings or a proposal to pitch a new project to your boss, it is important to understand the structure and purpose of these documents to effectively communicate your message.

In this chapter, we will discuss the key elements of reports and proposals, their purposes, and how to structure them effectively.

Reports: A report is a written document that provides information about a specific topic. It is usually written for a specific audience and has a defined structure. Reports are often used to communicate research findings, analysis, and recommendations.

The purpose of a report is to inform the reader about a specific topic, provide a detailed analysis of the information gathered, and make recommendations based on the analysis. Reports can be used to make decisions, plan strategies, and evaluate the success of a project.

Proposal: A proposal is a written document that outlines a specific plan or idea for a project, product, or service. Proposals are often used to pitch ideas to clients or to secure funding from investors.

The purpose of a proposal is to persuade the reader to take action on a specific idea or project. A good proposal should clearly define the problem or need that the proposal aims to address, provide a detailed plan of action, and demonstrate the potential benefits of the proposed idea or project.

Structure of a Report: Reports typically have a standard structure that includes the following sections:

1. Title Page: This includes the title of the report, the name of the author, the date of submission, and other relevant information.

2. Table of Contents: This lists the sections and subsections of the report, with page numbers for easy reference.

3. Introduction: This provides an overview of the report, including its purpose, scope, and any background information necessary to understand the topic.

4. Body: This is the main section of the report, where the research findings and analysis are presented. The body is often divided into sections and subsections, with headings and subheadings to make it easier to follow.

5. Conclusion: This summarizes the key findings and recommendations of the report.

6. References: This lists the sources cited in the report, using a standard citation format.

Structure of a Proposal: Proposals typically have a standard structure that includes the following sections:

1. Title Page: This includes the title of the proposal, the name of the author, the date of submission, and other relevant information.

2. Table of Contents: This lists the sections and subsections of the proposal, with page numbers for easy reference.

3. Executive Summary: This provides an overview of the proposal, including the problem or need that the proposal aims to address, the proposed solution, and the potential benefits of the proposed idea or project.

4. Introduction: This provides background information on the problem or need that the proposal aims to address.

5. Body: This is the main section of the proposal, where the proposed solution and plan of action are presented in detail. The body is often divided into sections and subsections, with headings and subheadings to make it easier to follow.

6. Conclusion: This summarizes the key points of the proposal and makes a clear call to action.

7. Appendices: This includes any additional information that supports the proposal, such as charts, graphs, or other data.

In conclusion, writing effective reports and proposals is an important skill for professionals in many industries. By understanding the structure and purpose of these documents, you can effectively communicate your message to your target audience and achieve your goals.

Using Formal Language and Tone in Business Writing

When it comes to business writing, the language and tone you use can make a big difference in how your message is received. Using a formal language and tone can help establish credibility, convey professionalism, and show respect for the reader. In this section, we'll discuss some tips for using formal language and tone in your business writing.

1. Avoid slang and informal language Using slang or informal language can make your writing sound unprofessional and undermine your credibility. Stick to formal language that is appropriate for the context.

2. Use proper grammar and punctuation Proper grammar and punctuation are essential in business writing. They help ensure that your message is clear and easy to understand. Use standard English grammar and punctuation rules and double-check your work for errors.

3. Avoid contractions Contractions are a common feature of informal language, but they have no place in formal business writing. Use the full form of words instead of contractions, such as "cannot" instead of "can't."

4. Write in the third person Writing in the third person can make your writing sound more objective and

professional. Avoid using the first person (I, we) or the second person (you) in formal business writing.

5. Use polite and courteous language Using polite and courteous language is essential in business writing. Be sure to use appropriate salutations and closing phrases, such as "Dear Sir/Madam" and "Yours faithfully," to show respect for the reader.

6. Use professional titles and job descriptions When referring to people in your business writing, use their professional titles and job descriptions. This shows respect and helps clarify roles and responsibilities.

7. Avoid emotive language Emotive language is language that is designed to create an emotional response in the reader. Avoid using emotive language in business writing as it can make your writing sound biased and unprofessional.

In conclusion, using formal language and tone in business writing is essential for establishing credibility, conveying professionalism, and showing respect for the reader. By following these tips, you can improve the quality of your business writing and increase its impact.

Formatting Your Report or Proposal for Maximum Clarity

When writing a report or proposal, it is essential to ensure that your document is formatted in a way that is easy to read and understand. Proper formatting not only makes your document more visually appealing but also helps to organize your ideas in a way that makes sense. In this section, we will discuss the key formatting elements to consider when writing reports and proposals.

Title Page The title page is the first page of your report or proposal and serves as the cover. It should include the following information:

- The title of your report or proposal

- Your name and the names of any co-authors

- The date of submission

- The name of the organization or company to which the document is being submitted

Table of Contents A table of contents is a list of the sections and headings in your report or proposal, along with their page numbers. It provides a roadmap for the reader, making it easier to navigate through the document. The table of contents should be formatted with clear headings and subheadings that reflect the structure of the document.

Executive Summary The executive summary is a brief overview of the report or proposal, usually one or two pages long. It should include the purpose of the document, key findings, and recommendations. The executive summary should be written in a clear and concise language, free from jargon and technical terms.

Introduction The introduction provides the context for the report or proposal, explaining why the document was written and what it aims to achieve. It should provide the reader with a clear understanding of the purpose and scope of the document.

Main Body The main body of your report or proposal should be organized into sections and subsections, each with a clear heading. It should present your research or analysis in a logical and coherent manner, supporting your arguments with evidence and examples.

Conclusion The conclusion should summarize the main points of the report or proposal and restate the recommendations. It should also emphasize the significance of the findings and suggest areas for further research or action.

References If you have used sources in your research, it is important to include a list of references at the end of your report or proposal. The references should be formatted in a consistent and standard style, such as APA or MLA.

Appendices If you have additional material that supports your arguments or findings, such as charts, graphs, or tables, you can include them in appendices at the end of your report or proposal. The appendices should be labeled clearly and referenced in the main body of the document.

Formatting Tips Here are some tips to ensure that your report or proposal is formatted for maximum clarity:

- Use headings and subheadings to break up your document into sections.

- Use bullet points and numbered lists to highlight key points.

- Use white space to make your document more visually appealing.

- Use a font that is easy to read, such as Times New Roman or Arial, and a font size of 12pt.

- Use consistent formatting throughout the document, such as margins, line spacing, and paragraph indentation.

- Use page numbers to make it easier for readers to navigate your document.

By following these formatting guidelines, you can make your report or proposal more readable and impactful, increasing the chances of your ideas being understood and accepted.

Editing and Proofreading Your Writing for Errors and Clarity

When it comes to business writing, editing and proofreading are critical steps that should never be skipped. Even the most brilliant ideas can be lost if they are not communicated clearly and correctly. In this section, we will explore the importance of editing and proofreading, the techniques you can use to improve your editing skills, and the common mistakes to avoid in the process.

Why Editing and Proofreading are Important

Editing and proofreading are essential steps in the writing process. They help to ensure that your message is clear and concise, and that your writing is free of errors. Some of the reasons why editing and proofreading are important include:

1. Improving Clarity: Editing and proofreading can help you to eliminate unnecessary words and phrases, and to restructure your sentences for maximum clarity. This can make your writing easier to understand, and help your readers to follow your argument more easily.

2. Correcting Errors: Editing and proofreading can help you to correct any grammatical, spelling, or punctuation errors that might detract from the clarity of your writing. Correcting these errors can help to ensure that your writing

is taken seriously and that your readers understand what you are trying to say.

3. Enhancing Credibility: When your writing is clear, concise, and error-free, it enhances your credibility as a writer. This can help to build trust with your readers and make them more likely to take your ideas seriously.

Techniques for Effective Editing and Proofreading

Effective editing and proofreading require more than just a quick read-through. Here are some techniques you can use to improve your editing skills:

1. Take a Break: Before you start editing, take a break from your writing. This can help you to approach your work with fresh eyes and a new perspective.

2. Read Aloud: Reading your work aloud can help you to identify awkward phrasing, repetition, and other issues that might be difficult to spot when reading silently.

3. Use Spell Check: While spell check is not foolproof, it can help you to catch spelling errors that might otherwise slip by.

4. Check for Consistency: Make sure that you are using consistent formatting, spelling, and punctuation throughout your document.

5. Get Feedback: Ask a colleague or friend to read over your work and provide feedback. This can help you to identify areas where your writing could be improved.

Common Mistakes to Avoid

Even with the best editing and proofreading techniques, it is still possible to make mistakes. Here are some common mistakes to avoid:

1. Relying Too Heavily on Spell Check: While spell check can be a useful tool, it is not foolproof. Always double-check your work for errors that might have slipped through.

2. Overlooking Small Errors: Even small errors, such as a misplaced comma or a misspelled word, can detract from the clarity of your writing. Make sure to check for these types of errors.

3. Failing to Read Your Work Aloud: Reading your work aloud can help you to identify awkward phrasing, repetition, and other issues that might be difficult to spot when reading silently.

4. Rushing: Editing and proofreading require time and attention. Rushing through these steps can lead to errors and oversights.

Conclusion

Editing and proofreading are critical steps in the writing process, and can help to ensure that your message is clear, concise, and error-free. By using effective editing techniques, avoiding common mistakes, and taking the time to carefully review your work, you can improve your business writing and enhance your credibility as a writer.

Chapter 4: Communicating in Social Situations Using Appropriate Language and Tone in Social Situations

Social situations require a different set of communication skills than professional or academic situations. In social situations, the goal is to build relationships, connect with others, and enjoy the company of others. Using appropriate language and tone is critical to achieving these goals. In this chapter, we will discuss the importance of using appropriate language and tone in social situations and provide tips on how to do so effectively.

Why Appropriate Language and Tone is Important in Social Situations:

Using appropriate language and tone in social situations is important for several reasons:

1. Building Relationships: Building relationships is the primary goal of social communication. Using appropriate language and tone helps create a positive impression and helps establish a connection with others.

2. Avoiding Misunderstandings: Social situations can be informal, and people may use language that is not appropriate in all situations. Using inappropriate language and tone can lead to misunderstandings and hurt feelings.

3. Respect and Courtesy: Using appropriate language and tone in social situations is a sign of respect and courtesy. It shows that you value the other person and care about their feelings.

Tips for Using Appropriate Language and Tone in Social Situations:

1. Be Mindful of Your Audience: Consider who you are talking to and what their expectations may be. The language and tone you use will differ depending on whether you are talking to a friend, a family member, or someone you have just met.

2. Avoid Offensive Language: Avoid using language that is offensive or derogatory. This includes racial slurs, sexist language, and derogatory terms.

3. Use Appropriate Language for the Situation: Use appropriate language for the situation. For example, using slang may be appropriate with friends, but not in a business setting or with someone you do not know well.

4. Tone: Pay attention to your tone of voice. Use a friendly and engaging tone to help build relationships. Avoid sounding too serious or too casual, as this can come across as insincere.

5. Body Language: Pay attention to your body language. Make eye contact, smile, and use appropriate gestures to show that you are engaged in the conversation.

Conclusion:

Using appropriate language and tone in social situations is essential for building relationships, avoiding misunderstandings, and showing respect and courtesy. By being mindful of your audience, avoiding offensive language, using appropriate language for the situation, paying attention to your tone and body language, you can effectively communicate in social situations and enjoy the company of others.

Understanding the Cultural Context of English Language Use

Language is more than just a tool for communication. It is a reflection of a person's cultural identity, beliefs, and values. Therefore, to communicate effectively in English, one must understand the cultural context in which the language is used.

English is a global language and is spoken by millions of people around the world. However, English speakers from different countries and cultures may have different ways of using the language. For example, the English spoken in the United States may differ from the English spoken in the United Kingdom or Australia.

To understand the cultural context of English language use, it is important to be aware of the following:

1. Regional Variations: English is spoken in different regions around the world, and each region may have its own variations in terms of pronunciation, vocabulary, and grammar. For example, British English and American English have some differences in spelling and pronunciation. Similarly, Indian English and Nigerian English may have variations in vocabulary and sentence structure.

2. Social Context: The way English is used may also depend on the social context. For example, the language used

in a formal setting, such as a business meeting or academic conference, may be different from the language used in a casual social gathering. Social factors such as age, gender, and socio-economic status may also influence the language used.

3. Cultural Values and Beliefs: Cultural values and beliefs play a significant role in shaping the way English is used. For example, in some cultures, indirect communication may be preferred, while in others, direct communication may be more common. Similarly, some cultures place a higher value on politeness and respect in language use, while others may prioritize efficiency and directness.

To communicate effectively in English, it is important to be aware of these cultural differences and adapt one's language use accordingly. Some tips for communicating in English in a culturally sensitive way include:

1. Be aware of regional variations in English and adjust your language use accordingly.

2. Consider the social context in which you are communicating and adjust your language use to suit the situation.

3. Respect cultural values and beliefs, and try to communicate in a way that is sensitive to these differences.

4. Avoid making assumptions about a person's cultural background based on their language use.

5. Seek feedback and ask for clarification if you are unsure about the meaning of something or if you feel that you may have caused offense.

In summary, understanding the cultural context of English language use is essential for effective communication. By being aware of regional variations, social context, and cultural values and beliefs, one can communicate in a way that is sensitive and respectful to others.

Avoiding Common Social Communication Mistakes in English

In social situations, effective communication is crucial to building and maintaining relationships. Communication mistakes can lead to misunderstandings, hurt feelings, and even damage to one's reputation. While non-native English speakers may face additional challenges in social communication, there are certain common mistakes that anyone can make regardless of their language background. In this section, we will discuss some common social communication mistakes in English and how to avoid them.

1. Interrupting others

One of the most common social communication mistakes is interrupting others while they are speaking. Interrupting can be seen as disrespectful and may give the impression that one is not interested in what the other person has to say. To avoid interrupting, it's important to practice active listening. This means focusing on the speaker's words and body language, and waiting for a natural pause before responding. If you do need to interrupt, apologize and explain why it's necessary.

2. Dominating the conversation

Another common mistake is dominating the conversation, where one person talks excessively and doesn't allow others to contribute. This can be seen as rude and selfish behavior. To avoid dominating the conversation, try to be aware of the amount of time you are speaking and allow others to speak as well. If you notice that someone is not contributing, ask them for their opinion or encourage them to speak.

3. Using inappropriate language

Using inappropriate language can also lead to communication breakdowns in social situations. This includes using profanity, slang, or offensive language. To avoid using inappropriate language, it's important to be aware of the context and the people you are speaking with. If you are unsure about the appropriateness of a certain word or phrase, it's better to err on the side of caution and avoid using it.

4. Making assumptions

Assuming that one understands what another person is thinking or feeling can also lead to communication mistakes. It's important to remember that everyone has their own perspective and experiences, and it's not always possible to know what someone else is thinking or feeling. To avoid making assumptions, ask open-ended questions and be willing to listen to the other person's point of view.

5. Not showing interest or engagement

Finally, not showing interest or engagement in the conversation can also be seen as a social communication mistake. This includes not making eye contact, fidgeting, or appearing distracted. To avoid this mistake, try to be fully present in the conversation and show interest in what the other person is saying. This can be done by making eye contact, nodding, asking questions, and providing feedback.

In conclusion, effective communication in social situations requires awareness of common communication mistakes and strategies to avoid them. By practicing active listening, allowing others to contribute, using appropriate language, avoiding assumptions, and showing interest and engagement, anyone can improve their social communication skills in English.

Building Confidence and Fluency in Social Communication Situations

Effective communication is not just about knowing the language, it is also about having the confidence to use it in different situations. In social situations, being able to express yourself fluently and with confidence can make all the difference in forming relationships and making friends. In this chapter, we will explore some tips and strategies for building confidence and fluency in social communication situations.

1. Practice, Practice, Practice

One of the most effective ways to build confidence and fluency in social communication situations is through practice. The more you practice speaking, the more comfortable and confident you will become. Seek out opportunities to speak English in social situations, such as joining a conversation club, attending social events, or even practicing with friends.

2. Focus on Fluency

In social situations, it is more important to focus on fluency than accuracy. Don't worry too much about making mistakes or using perfect grammar. The key is to be able to express yourself clearly and fluently, so that others can understand what you are saying. By focusing on fluency, you can build your confidence and start to feel more comfortable speaking English in social situations.

3. Learn and Use Common Idioms and Expressions

One way to improve your fluency is to learn and use common idioms and expressions. These are phrases that are commonly used in English, and can add color and depth to your language. By learning and using idioms and expressions, you can sound more like a native speaker, and build your confidence in social situations.

4. Use Body Language

In social situations, your body language can be just as important as your spoken language. Use eye contact, facial expressions, and gestures to help convey your message. Pay attention to the body language of others, and respond accordingly. Using body language can help you feel more confident and comfortable in social situations, and can also help you better understand the messages of others.

5. Listen Carefully

Listening is a crucial part of effective communication, especially in social situations. When you listen carefully, you can better understand the context and the messages being conveyed. This can help you respond more appropriately and build stronger relationships. Practice active listening by focusing on what the other person is saying, and asking questions to clarify if needed.

6. Be Prepared

If you know you are going to be in a social situation where you will need to speak English, it can help to be prepared. Think about possible topics of conversation, and practice discussing them in advance. This can help you feel more confident and fluent when the time comes to speak.

7. Have Fun

Finally, remember to have fun! Learning a new language and communicating in social situations can be challenging, but it can also be very rewarding. Don't take yourself too seriously, and don't be afraid to make mistakes. Focus on enjoying the process of learning and communicating, and you will find that your confidence and fluency will grow naturally over time.

Conclusion

Building confidence and fluency in social communication situations can be a challenging but rewarding process. By practicing, focusing on fluency, using idioms and expressions, using body language, listening carefully, being prepared, and having fun, you can build your confidence and fluency and feel more comfortable speaking English in social situations. Remember, effective communication is not just about the language you use, it's also about the confidence and fluency with which you use it.

Chapter 5: Effective Communication in the Workplace
Understanding the Workplace Communication Context

Effective communication in the workplace is an essential skill for success in any organization. To communicate effectively, it is essential to understand the communication context in the workplace. The context includes the organizational culture, communication channels, and the diversity of the workforce. Understanding the communication context helps employees communicate better with each other and promotes a positive work environment. In this section, we will discuss the different aspects of workplace communication context that can influence effective communication.

Organizational Culture Organizational culture refers to the shared values, beliefs, and behaviors that define the workplace. The culture can impact how employees communicate with each other and the organization's external stakeholders. In some organizations, the culture may emphasize a hierarchical approach to communication, while others may promote open and collaborative communication. Understanding the organizational culture is essential to communicate effectively in the workplace. Employees should be aware of the company's culture, including the preferred communication style, tone, and language.

Communication Channels Communication channels refer to the different methods used to convey information in the workplace. In most organizations, there are different communication channels such as email, instant messaging, phone calls, and face-to-face communication. Different communication channels may be appropriate for different situations. For instance, email may be suitable for formal communication, while instant messaging may be more suitable for quick and informal communication. Understanding the communication channels in the workplace is crucial to selecting the most appropriate channel for a particular communication.

Workforce Diversity Workforce diversity refers to the differences among employees in an organization. Diversity can include differences in age, race, gender, language, and culture. In a diverse workforce, it is essential to communicate in a way that respects and values differences. Employees should be aware of cultural differences, language barriers, and other factors that may impact communication. Being sensitive to diversity can help employees avoid misunderstandings and promote a positive work environment.

In conclusion, understanding the workplace communication context is crucial to communicate effectively in the workplace. Employees should be aware of the organizational culture, communication channels, and workforce diversity. Effective communication in the workplace can help employees build positive relationships, solve problems, and achieve organizational goals.

Using Appropriate Language and Tone with Colleagues and Supervisors

Effective communication in the workplace is crucial for building strong relationships with colleagues, supervisors, and clients. One important aspect of effective communication is using appropriate language and tone in your interactions with others. In this section, we will discuss some guidelines for using appropriate language and tone with colleagues and supervisors.

1. Use Professional Language

It is important to use professional language in your workplace communication. This means using language that is appropriate for a business setting and avoiding slang or overly casual language. Professional language can help you come across as more credible and trustworthy to your colleagues and supervisors. It can also help to avoid misunderstandings or offense caused by inappropriate language.

2. Tailor Your Language to the Situation

It is important to tailor your language to the situation you are in. Different communication situations may require different levels of formality or informality. For example, you may use more formal language when communicating with your supervisor or when writing a formal email, but more informal language when chatting with colleagues in the break room. Pay attention to the context of your communication and adjust your language accordingly.

3. Be Mindful of Tone

Tone is the way in which you express your attitude or emotions through your language. It is important to be mindful of your tone when communicating with colleagues and supervisors. Your tone can influence how your message is received and can impact your relationships with others. Make an effort to communicate in a positive and respectful tone, even if you are addressing a difficult topic or disagreement.

4. Be Clear and Concise

Using appropriate language and tone also means being clear and concise in your communication. Avoid using unnecessarily complex language or technical jargon that may be difficult for others to understand. Use clear and concise language to ensure that your message is easily understood and that there is no confusion.

5. Be Polite and Respectful

Politeness and respect are essential for effective communication in the workplace. Show respect for your colleagues and supervisors by using polite language, listening actively, and acknowledging their contributions.

Use appropriate titles and salutations when addressing colleagues and supervisors. Avoid interrupting others or speaking over them during meetings or discussions.

6. Be Sensitive to Cultural Differences

In a diverse workplace, it is important to be sensitive to cultural differences in communication. Be aware that language and tone may be interpreted differently by people from different cultural backgrounds. Take the time to learn about the cultural norms of your colleagues and supervisors to avoid misunderstandings or offense caused by inappropriate language or tone.

7. Be Open to Feedback

Finally, be open to feedback from colleagues and supervisors about your communication style. Ask for feedback on your language and tone, and be willing to make changes or adjustments as needed. This can help you to continually improve your communication skills and build stronger relationships with those around you.

In conclusion, using appropriate language and tone in your workplace communication is essential for effective communication and building strong relationships with colleagues and supervisors. By following these guidelines, you can communicate in a way that is professional, clear, and respectful, while avoiding misunderstandings or offense caused by inappropriate language or tone.

Providing Constructive Feedback in a Professional Manner

Providing constructive feedback is an essential part of effective communication in the workplace. Constructive feedback helps employees grow and develop, enhances their job performance, and improves the overall productivity of the team. In this section, we will discuss the key elements of providing constructive feedback in a professional manner.

1. Be specific and objective The first step to providing constructive feedback is to be specific and objective. Instead of making general comments, provide specific examples of the behavior or situation that needs improvement. This helps the employee understand exactly what needs to be addressed and how it can be improved. Additionally, being objective ensures that the feedback is not based on personal biases or opinions.

2. Focus on behavior, not personality When providing feedback, it is important to focus on the behavior, not the person. Avoid making personal attacks or criticisms and instead, focus on the actions or behaviors that need to be changed. This approach ensures that the feedback is constructive and helps the employee improve, rather than causing them to feel defensive or attacked.

3. Use the sandwich approach The sandwich approach is a popular technique for providing constructive feedback. This involves starting with a positive comment, followed by the area of improvement, and ending with another positive comment. This approach ensures that the feedback is balanced and provides the employee with both constructive criticism and encouragement.

4. Be timely Providing timely feedback is crucial to ensuring that the employee understands the situation and can make the necessary changes. Avoid waiting too long to provide feedback, as it may become irrelevant or difficult for the employee to address.

5. Be empathetic Providing constructive feedback can be challenging, and it is important to be empathetic when delivering the message. Put yourself in the employee's shoes and consider how they may feel about the situation. Approach the feedback with kindness and respect, and avoid using a harsh or critical tone.

6. Provide actionable steps When providing feedback, it is important to provide actionable steps for improvement. Work with the employee to develop a plan for addressing the issue, and provide support and resources to help them make the necessary changes.

7. Follow up Following up after providing feedback is essential to ensure that the employee is making progress and that the issue is being addressed. Schedule a follow-up meeting or check-in to discuss any changes or improvements that have been made and provide further guidance if necessary.

In conclusion, providing constructive feedback is an essential component of effective communication in the workplace. By being specific, objective, and empathetic, and by using the sandwich approach and providing actionable steps, you can help employees grow and develop, improve their job performance, and contribute to the overall success of the team.

Building Effective Relationships in the Workplace

Building effective relationships in the workplace is an essential component of successful communication in any organization. When employees work together effectively, they can achieve shared goals and create a positive work environment. This chapter will explore the importance of building effective relationships in the workplace, as well as provide strategies for doing so.

Importance of Building Effective Relationships

Effective relationships in the workplace help to create a positive working environment. This can lead to increased productivity, job satisfaction, and employee retention. When employees feel comfortable and supported at work, they are more likely to be engaged and committed to their job, which can lead to better overall job performance. Effective relationships also contribute to effective teamwork, which is critical in achieving organizational goals.

Strategies for Building Effective Relationships

There are several strategies that employees can use to build effective relationships in the workplace:

1. Communicate Openly and Honestly

Open and honest communication is the foundation of effective relationships. Employees should communicate their thoughts, feelings, and concerns to their colleagues and supervisors in a respectful and professional manner. This can help to prevent misunderstandings and build trust between colleagues.

2. Listen Actively

Active listening is an important skill for building effective relationships. When employees listen actively, they demonstrate that they value their colleagues' perspectives and opinions. They should listen to their colleagues' concerns and offer support when appropriate. Active listening also involves asking questions to clarify understanding and to show interest in what the other person is saying.

3. Show Respect and Appreciation

Showing respect and appreciation for colleagues is another important strategy for building effective relationships. Employees should be respectful of their colleagues' opinions, even if they do not agree with them. They should also take the time to show appreciation for their colleagues' contributions and accomplishments.

4. Build Trust

Trust is essential for building effective relationships in the workplace. Employees can build trust by being reliable, honest, and consistent in their behavior. They should also be willing to admit their mistakes and take responsibility for their actions.

5. Collaborate Effectively

Collaboration is critical for building effective relationships in the workplace. Employees should work together to achieve shared goals and share responsibility for project outcomes. They should also be willing to compromise when necessary and to be flexible in their approach.

6. Manage Conflict Constructively

Conflict is a natural part of any workplace, but it can be managed constructively. Employees should learn to express their concerns and disagreements in a respectful and professional manner. They should also be willing to listen to their colleagues' perspectives and work together to find a solution that meets everyone's needs.

7. Foster a Positive Work Environment

Creating a positive work environment is essential for building effective relationships in the workplace. Employees should be supportive of their colleagues and celebrate their successes. They should also be willing to lend a helping hand when needed and to show empathy when their colleagues are experiencing difficulties.

Conclusion

Building effective relationships in the workplace is essential for creating a positive work environment and achieving shared goals. Open and honest communication, active listening, respect and appreciation, trust, effective collaboration, constructive conflict management, and fostering a positive work environment are all critical strategies for building effective relationships. When employees work together effectively, they can create a culture of collaboration and support, which can lead to increased productivity, job satisfaction, and employee retention.

Chapter 6: Understanding and Using Idiomatic Language

Understanding the Role of Idioms in English Language Use

Idioms are a unique feature of the English language and are commonly used in everyday speech, writing, and communication. An idiom is a phrase or expression whose meaning cannot be deduced from the literal definition of its individual words. Instead, it is an expression whose meaning is understood by a group of people and is used in a specific context. Idiomatic expressions add richness and depth to language, but they can also be confusing and difficult to understand for non-native English speakers.

Origins of Idioms

Many idiomatic expressions have their origins in historical events, cultural traditions, or ancient stories. For example, the idiom "to have a skeleton in the closet" means to have a secret that you do not want other people to know. The phrase originates from the practice of hiding dead bodies in closets during the time of plagues in Europe. Similarly, the expression "to let the cat out of the bag" means to reveal a secret. Its origins can be traced back to the practice of fraudsters selling pigs in a bag, but instead of a pig, they would put a cat. If the buyer did not check the contents of the bag, they would unknowingly purchase a cat.

The Importance of Idioms in Communication

Idioms are an integral part of the English language and are used frequently in everyday communication, including social and professional contexts. They can be used to convey complex ideas in a concise manner, add color to a conversation, or create a more conversational tone. Using idioms can also help to establish a rapport with the listener or reader by demonstrating a shared cultural knowledge and understanding.

Idioms can also play a role in establishing a speaker's fluency and competence in the English language. The ability to use idioms correctly and appropriately shows a deeper understanding of the language beyond its literal meaning. For non-native English speakers, learning idiomatic expressions is an important aspect of mastering the language and improving fluency.

Challenges of Using Idioms

While idioms can be a powerful tool in communication, they can also present significant challenges for non-native English speakers. The complexity and ambiguity of idiomatic expressions can lead to confusion, misunderstandings, and even offense if used incorrectly or inappropriately.

One of the main challenges in using idioms is that their meaning cannot be deduced from the literal definition of the words. Instead, their meaning is often based on cultural knowledge or context. As a result, idiomatic expressions may not translate well to other languages or cultures, which can lead to difficulties for non-native English speakers in understanding and using them appropriately.

Another challenge of idioms is that their usage can vary based on regional dialects or accents. For example, an idiom that is commonly used in British English may not be used in American English, or its meaning may be different. This can make it difficult for non-native English speakers to navigate the nuances of idiomatic expressions in different English-speaking contexts.

Tips for Using Idioms Appropriately

To use idioms correctly and effectively, it is important to understand their context and usage. Here are some tips for using idioms appropriately:

1. Learn idiomatic expressions in context: Understanding the cultural context of idiomatic expressions is essential for using them correctly. Rather than simply memorizing idioms and their definitions, try to learn them in

context by reading or listening to conversations in which they are used.

2. Use idioms sparingly: Overuse of idioms can make communication difficult for non-native English speakers or those who are not familiar with the specific idiom. Use idioms sparingly and only when they add value to the conversation or writing.

3. Be mindful of cultural differences: Idiomatic expressions can have different meanings or usage in different cultures. Be aware of these differences and avoid using idiomatic expressions that could be considered offensive or inappropriate in certain cultures. For example, the idiom "spill the beans" may be perfectly acceptable in Western cultures to mean revealing a secret, but could be confusing or even offensive in other cultures where beans may not hold the same cultural significance. Additionally, idioms can vary in their popularity and usage in different regions or countries, so it's important to consider the context and audience before using them.

1. Practice using idiomatic language: Like any other aspect of language learning, using idiomatic expressions requires practice. Start by incorporating a few common idioms into your daily conversations or writing, and gradually expand your knowledge and usage. Reading

English literature or watching English-speaking media can also be a helpful way to expose yourself to a variety of idiomatic expressions in context.

2. Seek feedback and clarification: Don't be afraid to ask native English speakers for feedback or clarification when using or encountering idiomatic language. They can provide valuable insight into the appropriateness or meaning of idioms in different contexts, and can help you refine your usage and understanding.

By understanding the role of idiomatic language in English and practicing their usage in appropriate contexts, learners can improve their overall fluency and comprehension of the language.

Identifying Common Idioms and Their Meanings

Idioms are a unique aspect of the English language, and mastering them can greatly improve one's ability to communicate effectively. An idiom is a phrase or expression that has a figurative meaning that is different from the literal meaning of the words used. These expressions are often used in informal settings and can be difficult for non-native speakers to understand.

To identify and understand idiomatic language, it's helpful to start by learning some of the most common idioms used in everyday conversation. Some of the most commonly used idioms include:

1. "Break a leg" - This expression is often used to wish someone good luck. It is commonly used in the entertainment industry and has origins in the theatre world.

2. "Bite the bullet" - This expression means to face a difficult or unpleasant situation with courage and resolve.

3. "Kick the bucket" - This is a euphemism for dying.

4. "The ball is in your court" - This expression means that it's up to someone to take action or make a decision.

5. "Cost an arm and a leg" - This expression means that something is very expensive.

6. "A piece of cake" - This expression means that something is very easy to do.

7. "Let the cat out of the bag" - This expression means to reveal a secret.

8. "Hit the nail on the head" - This expression means to identify the exact problem or issue.

9. "On the same page" - This expression means that people are in agreement or have the same understanding.

10. "Spill the beans" - This expression means to reveal a secret or confidential information.

Understanding the meaning of these and other idioms is important for effective communication in English. However, it's important to note that idioms can vary by region and culture, so it's important to be aware of these differences.

To identify the meanings of idioms, it can be helpful to look at the context in which they are used. Often, idioms will be used in a sentence that makes it clear what the intended meaning is. For example, if someone says "I'm feeling under the weather today," it's clear from the context that they are not feeling well, even though the literal meaning of the words might not suggest that.

Another way to identify the meaning of idioms is to use online resources, such as idiom dictionaries and websites that explain the meanings of common idioms. These resources can be especially helpful for non-native speakers

who are just starting to learn English and may not be familiar with many idiomatic expressions.

In addition to learning the meanings of idioms, it's also important to understand their usage. Idioms are often used in informal conversations, so they may not be appropriate in more formal settings, such as business meetings or academic presentations. It's important to be mindful of the context in which idioms are used to avoid any confusion or misunderstandings.

Overall, identifying common idioms and their meanings is an important step in mastering the English language. By learning these expressions, non-native speakers can better understand and communicate with English speakers, and avoid any confusion or misunderstandings that may arise from using idiomatic language inappropriately.

Using Idiomatic Language Appropriately and Effectively

While idiomatic language can add color and personality to your writing and speech, it's important to use idioms appropriately and effectively in order to avoid confusion or misunderstandings. Here are some tips for using idiomatic language effectively:

1. Understand the meaning: Before using an idiom, make sure you understand its meaning and usage. Look up the definition and read examples to get a sense of how it's used in context. This will help you avoid using an idiom incorrectly or in the wrong situation.

2. Consider your audience: Be mindful of your audience when using idiomatic language. Some idioms may be more familiar to certain groups or cultures, so it's important to use idioms that are appropriate and easily understood by your intended audience.

3. Use idioms sparingly: While idiomatic language can be fun and engaging, it's important not to overuse them. Using too many idioms can be overwhelming for your audience and may come across as insincere or unprofessional.

4. Avoid mixed metaphors: A mixed metaphor is when two or more idiomatic expressions are combined in a way

that doesn't make sense. For example, "Don't count your chickens before they hatch" and "Don't put all your eggs in one basket" are two different idioms that shouldn't be mixed together. Mixing idioms can confuse your audience and make your message less effective.

5. Use idioms in context: It's important to use idioms in a way that makes sense in the context of what you're saying or writing. If an idiom doesn't fit naturally in your sentence, it may be better to use a different phrase or expression.

6. Practice using idiomatic language: The more you practice using idiomatic language, the more comfortable and confident you will become. Practice using idioms in writing and speech, and ask for feedback from others to help you improve.

In conclusion, using idiomatic language can add personality and interest to your writing and speech, but it's important to use them appropriately and effectively. Understanding the meaning of idioms, considering your audience, using idioms sparingly, avoiding mixed metaphors, using idioms in context, and practicing using idiomatic language are all important aspects of using idioms effectively. By following these tips, you can use idiomatic language to enhance your communication skills and make a lasting impression on your audience.

Developing Confidence and Fluency in Using Idiomatic Language

Using idiomatic language can be a great way to add depth and complexity to your speech or writing. However, it can also be a source of anxiety for non-native speakers of English. Here are some tips for developing confidence and fluency in using idiomatic language:

1. Start with the basics: Begin by learning common idioms that are used in everyday conversation. This can include expressions such as "break a leg," "piece of cake," or "hit the nail on the head." Practice using them in context until they become second nature to you.

2. Watch and listen: Exposure to authentic English language use is crucial for developing confidence in using idiomatic language. Watch TV shows or movies, listen to podcasts or audiobooks, and pay attention to how native speakers use idioms in different contexts.

3. Keep a journal: Start a journal where you can record idiomatic expressions that you come across in your reading or listening. Write down the context in which the expression was used and its meaning. This will help you remember the expressions and provide you with a reference when you need to use them.

4. Use idioms in conversation: Practice using idioms in conversation with native speakers or other non-native speakers who are also learning English. This will give you an opportunity to practice in a low-stakes environment and receive feedback on your usage.

5. Contextualize: Remember that idioms are often highly contextual and cannot be used in all situations. Pay attention to the context in which idioms are used and avoid using them in inappropriate situations.

6. Be aware of cultural differences: As mentioned in the previous section, idioms can have different meanings or usage in different cultures. Be aware of these differences and avoid using idioms that may be offensive or inappropriate in certain contexts.

7. Don't force it: Don't feel like you have to use idioms in every sentence or conversation. It's better to use idioms sparingly and appropriately than to use them incorrectly or excessively.

Overall, developing confidence and fluency in using idiomatic language takes time and practice. However, with exposure to authentic language use, an understanding of cultural differences, and a willingness to learn and make mistakes, you can become a more confident and effective communicator in English.

Chapter 7: Communicating in Academic Contexts Understanding the Expectations and Norms of Academic Communication

Effective communication in academic contexts involves a specific set of expectations and norms that differ from those in other contexts, such as social or workplace communication. In this chapter, we will discuss the expectations and norms of academic communication and provide tips for communicating effectively in academic contexts.

The Role of Clarity and Precision

One of the most important expectations in academic communication is clarity and precision. Academic writing is expected to be clear and precise to avoid any ambiguity or confusion. This is particularly important when presenting research findings or discussing complex theories. Ambiguous or imprecise language can lead to misinterpretation or confusion, which can undermine the credibility of the work.

The Use of Formal Language

Academic writing is expected to use formal language. This means avoiding colloquial language, contractions, and slang. The use of formal language demonstrates respect for the subject matter and the reader, as well as a level of professionalism. It is important to note that this does not mean academic writing should be overly complex or difficult to understand. Instead, it should be clear, concise, and accessible to the intended audience.

The Importance of Citations and Referencing

In academic writing, it is crucial to give credit to the sources used. This is done through the use of citations and referencing. Proper citation and referencing show the reader that the work is based on sound research and that the writer has considered the ideas and findings of others. Failure to cite sources can lead to accusations of plagiarism, which can have serious consequences in academic contexts.

The Role of Evidence

Academic writing is based on evidence. This means that claims or arguments made in academic writing should be supported by evidence from credible sources. Evidence can take many forms, including empirical research, theoretical frameworks, or analysis of existing literature. The use of evidence demonstrates the writer's knowledge of the subject matter and their ability to critically analyze information.

The Importance of Critical Thinking

Academic communication also involves critical thinking. Critical thinking involves analyzing and evaluating information to make informed decisions or arguments. In academic writing, critical thinking is demonstrated through the ability to analyze and synthesize information, question assumptions, and draw logical conclusions based on evidence.

The Role of Feedback

Feedback is an integral part of academic communication. Academic writing often involves multiple rounds of feedback, including feedback from peers, professors, or editors. Feedback helps writers to refine their ideas, clarify their arguments, and identify any weaknesses in their work. Accepting and incorporating feedback is essential for improving the quality of academic writing.

Conclusion

Effective communication in academic contexts requires a thorough understanding of the expectations and norms of academic communication. These include the importance of clarity and precision, the use of formal language, the role of citations and referencing, the importance of evidence and critical thinking, and the role of feedback. By understanding and applying these expectations and norms, writers can effectively communicate their ideas and research findings to their intended audience.

Writing Clear and Concise Academic Papers and Essays

Academic writing can be a challenging task, especially for those who are new to it. Writing an academic paper or essay requires a specific set of skills and techniques to ensure that the content is clear, concise, and effective. In this section, we will discuss some tips and strategies to help you write clear and concise academic papers and essays.

1. Understand the assignment requirements: Before you start writing, it is essential to understand the assignment requirements. Read the instructions carefully, and make sure you understand what is expected of you. Ask your instructor if you have any questions.

2. Develop a clear thesis statement: A thesis statement is the main idea or argument that you will be making in your paper or essay. It should be clear, concise, and specific. Your thesis statement should be presented in the introductory paragraph of your paper.

3. Organize your thoughts: Organizing your thoughts is essential to ensure that your paper or essay is clear and concise. Create an outline that includes the main points you want to cover and the order in which you will present them.

4. Use clear and concise language: Use clear and concise language to convey your ideas. Avoid using complex

sentences or technical jargon that may confuse your readers. Keep your sentences short and to the point.

5. Provide evidence to support your arguments: Your arguments should be supported by evidence from credible sources. Use quotes, statistics, and examples to back up your claims.

6. Avoid redundancy: Avoid repeating the same points or ideas in your paper or essay. Be concise and get straight to the point.

7. Use transitional words and phrases: Transitional words and phrases can help you move smoothly from one idea to the next. Use words like "however," "nevertheless," "in addition," and "furthermore" to connect your ideas.

8. Revise and edit: Once you have written your paper or essay, take some time to revise and edit it. Read it aloud to check for clarity and flow. Check for spelling and grammatical errors.

9. Get feedback: It can be helpful to get feedback on your paper or essay from someone else. Ask a friend or classmate to read it and provide constructive criticism.

By following these tips and strategies, you can write clear and concise academic papers and essays that effectively communicate your ideas to your readers. Remember to start early and give yourself plenty of time to complete your assignments to ensure that you can revise and edit your work thoroughly.

Properly Citing Sources and Avoiding Plagiarism in Academic Writing

Properly citing sources and avoiding plagiarism is an essential aspect of academic writing. Plagiarism is the act of presenting someone else's work or ideas as your own, and it is considered academic dishonesty. Therefore, it is crucial to learn how to cite sources properly and avoid plagiarism in your academic writing.

There are different citation styles used in academic writing, including APA, MLA, Chicago, and Harvard. Each style has its specific rules and guidelines on how to cite sources. It is essential to learn the citation style required by your institution and use it consistently throughout your paper.

When citing sources, you should include in-text citations and a reference list or bibliography at the end of your paper. In-text citations provide brief information about the source you are citing and refer to the full citation in the reference list or bibliography. The reference list should include all sources cited in the paper, arranged in alphabetical order by the author's last name.

When citing sources, you should be careful to include all the necessary information, such as the author's name, the year of publication, the title of the article or book, the publisher, and the page numbers. Failing to include this information can result in an incomplete or incorrect citation, which can lead to accusations of plagiarism.

To avoid plagiarism, you should always give credit to the original author of the ideas, words, or concepts you use in your paper. This includes direct quotes, paraphrasing, and summarizing. Direct quotes should be enclosed in quotation marks and cited using in-text citations and the reference list or bibliography. When paraphrasing or summarizing, you should rephrase the original text in your own words and cite the source appropriately.

It is also important to be aware of the different types of plagiarism, such as self-plagiarism, patchwork plagiarism, and citation plagiarism. Self-plagiarism is the act of submitting the same paper or parts of a paper for multiple assignments without proper citation. Patchwork plagiarism is the act of combining multiple sources without proper citation to create a new paper. Citation plagiarism is the act of citing sources incorrectly or inaccurately.

In addition to citing sources properly and avoiding plagiarism, you should also use plagiarism detection tools to check your paper for unintentional plagiarism. These tools scan your paper for similarities with other sources and help you identify areas where you need to cite sources or rephrase the text.

In conclusion, proper citation and avoiding plagiarism are crucial aspects of academic writing. By learning the citation style required by your institution, including in-text citations and a reference list or bibliography, and giving credit to the original authors of the ideas you use, you can avoid plagiarism and ensure academic integrity in your writing.

Engaging in Productive Academic Discussions and Debates

One of the most important aspects of academic communication is engaging in productive discussions and debates. These types of interactions allow individuals to share ideas, challenge each other's beliefs, and ultimately arrive at a deeper understanding of a topic. However, engaging in productive discussions and debates requires a specific set of skills and strategies.

1. Preparation

Before engaging in a discussion or debate, it is important to be well-prepared. This includes having a thorough understanding of the topic at hand and any relevant background information. It can also be helpful to anticipate potential arguments or objections that may be raised by others in the discussion.

2. Active Listening

Active listening is an essential skill for engaging in productive discussions and debates. This means not only hearing what the other person is saying, but also making an effort to understand their perspective. It involves asking clarifying questions, summarizing what the other person has said, and acknowledging their point of view.

3. Respecting Different Opinions

In academic discussions and debates, it is inevitable that different opinions will be expressed. It is important to approach these differences with respect and an open mind. Avoid attacking or belittling someone for their beliefs, as this can shut down the discussion and make it more difficult to reach a productive outcome.

4. Constructive Criticism

Constructive criticism is a key component of productive discussions and debates. This means offering feedback in a way that is helpful and respectful. Avoid attacking or criticizing the individual, and instead focus on their arguments or ideas. It is also important to offer suggestions for improvement or alternative viewpoints.

5. Avoiding Logical Fallacies

Logical fallacies are common errors in reasoning that can derail a discussion or debate. These can include ad hominem attacks (attacking the individual instead of their arguments), strawman arguments (misrepresenting someone's position), and appeals to emotion (using emotions instead of reason to make an argument). It is important to be aware of these fallacies and avoid using them in discussions and debates.

6. Staying Calm and Objective

Finally, it is important to stay calm and objective during discussions and debates. Avoid getting overly emotional or defensive, as this can escalate the situation and make it more difficult to arrive at a productive outcome. Instead, focus on the facts and logic of the argument, and remain open to changing your perspective based on new information or insights.

In conclusion, engaging in productive academic discussions and debates requires a combination of preparation, active listening, respect for different opinions, constructive criticism, avoiding logical fallacies, and staying calm and objective. By developing these skills and strategies, individuals can become more effective communicators in academic contexts.

Conclusion

Summary of Key Points

The ability to communicate effectively is essential for success in both personal and professional life. In this guide, we have explored various aspects of communication in different contexts, including social, workplace, and academic settings. Throughout these chapters, we have covered several key points that are worth summarizing.

In the first chapter, we discussed the importance of effective communication skills, including active listening, nonverbal communication, and clarity in speech. We also discussed how to overcome common communication barriers, such as language differences and cultural misunderstandings.

In chapter two, we focused on building rapport and establishing trust in communication. We emphasized the importance of empathy, respect, and open-mindedness in creating positive relationships with others. We also explored strategies for managing conflict and resolving disputes in a constructive manner.

Chapter three focused on developing effective public speaking skills. We discussed the importance of preparation and practice, as well as techniques for engaging an audience and delivering a clear and concise message.

In chapter four, we explored communication in social situations, including how to use appropriate language and tone, understanding cultural differences, avoiding common mistakes, and building confidence and fluency.

Chapter five focused on effective communication in the workplace, including using appropriate language and tone with colleagues and supervisors, providing constructive feedback, and building effective relationships.

Chapter six discussed idiomatic language, including understanding the role of idioms, identifying common idioms and their meanings, and using idiomatic language appropriately and effectively.

Finally, in chapter seven, we discussed academic communication, including understanding the expectations and norms of academic writing, writing clear and concise academic papers and essays, properly citing sources and avoiding plagiarism, and engaging in productive academic discussions and debates.

Overall, effective communication is a multifaceted skill that requires practice and patience. By applying the strategies and techniques discussed in this guide, you can enhance your communication skills and achieve greater success in all aspects of your life. Remember to be mindful of your audience, listen actively, speak clearly and concisely, and approach communication with an open mind and a willingness to learn and grow. With these tools and a commitment to continuous improvement, you can become a more effective communicator and achieve your goals.

Practical Tips for Applying What You've Learned

Throughout this book, we've discussed various aspects of effective communication in different contexts, including social situations, the workplace, and academic settings. Now, it's time to put what you've learned into practice. Here are some practical tips for applying what you've learned:

1. Practice, practice, practice: The key to improving your communication skills is to practice as much as possible. This can involve speaking with native speakers, practicing with language partners, or simply speaking to yourself in English.

2. Be patient: Learning a new language takes time, and there will be times when you feel frustrated or discouraged. Remember to be patient with yourself and keep practicing.

3. Set goals: Setting goals can help you stay motivated and focused. For example, you might set a goal to learn a certain number of new idioms each week or to improve your pronunciation in a specific area.

4. Seek feedback: Ask native speakers or language teachers for feedback on your communication skills. This can help you identify areas for improvement and make adjustments accordingly.

5. Use technology: There are many online tools and resources that can help you improve your English communication skills, including language learning apps, pronunciation tools, and online language communities.

6. Stay up-to-date: Language use and cultural norms are constantly changing, so it's important to stay up-to-date on the latest trends and developments. Reading news articles, watching English-language TV shows and movies, and following English-speaking influencers on social media can all help you stay current.

7. Embrace mistakes: Don't be afraid to make mistakes when speaking or writing in English. Mistakes are a natural part of the learning process, and they can help you identify areas for improvement.

8. Have fun: Learning a new language should be a fun and rewarding experience. Find ways to make the learning process enjoyable, such as listening to music in English, watching funny YouTube videos, or playing language learning games.

By following these practical tips, you can continue to improve your English communication skills and become a more effective communicator in social, workplace, and academic contexts. Remember to stay motivated, be patient with yourself, and enjoy the learning process!

Further Resources for Improving Your English Language Skills

English is a constantly evolving language, and there is always more to learn. Even after reading this guide, you may still want to improve your skills. Fortunately, there are many resources available to help you continue to improve your English language abilities.

1. Online Courses: There are many online courses available that are designed to help people improve their English language skills. These courses can be accessed from anywhere, and many of them are free or low-cost. Some popular options include Duolingo, Rosetta Stone, and Babbel.

2. Tutoring Services: If you prefer one-on-one instruction, you may want to consider working with an English language tutor. There are many tutors available both online and in-person, and they can help you improve your reading, writing, listening, and speaking skills.

3. Language Exchange Programs: Language exchange programs are a great way to practice your English skills with native speakers. These programs allow you to connect with people from around the world who are also learning English, and you can help each other practice your language skills.

4. English Language Books: There are many great books available that can help you improve your English skills. Some popular options include "The Elements of Style" by William Strunk Jr. and E.B. White, "English Grammar in Use" by Raymond Murphy, and "The Blue Book of Grammar and Punctuation" by Jane Straus.

5. English Language Apps: There are many apps available that can help you practice your English language skills on the go. Some popular options include Grammarly, Quizlet, and FluentU.

6. English Language Meetup Groups: Joining an English language meetup group can be a great way to practice your language skills and meet new people. These groups typically meet in person, and they may focus on conversation practice, cultural exchange, or other language-related activities.

7. English Language Podcasts: Listening to English language podcasts can be a great way to improve your listening and comprehension skills. Some popular options include "This American Life," "Serial," and "TED Talks."

8. English Language Websites: There are many websites available that can help you improve your English skills. Some popular options include BBC Learning English, ESLgold.com, and EnglishCentral.com.

No matter what your level of proficiency is, there is always room for improvement when it comes to English language skills. By taking advantage of the many resources available, you can continue to grow and develop your skills, and become more confident and proficient in your communication abilities.

THE END

To help you better understand the language and concepts related to aging and older adults, below you will find a list of key terms and their definitions.

1. Fluency: The ability to speak or write a language easily, smoothly, and with confidence.

2. Idiomatic Language: Phrases or expressions that have a different meaning than what the individual words suggest, and are specific to a particular language or dialect.

3. Pronunciation: The way in which words are spoken or articulated.

4. Grammar: The set of rules that govern the structure of a language, including the arrangement of words, phrases, and clauses.

5. Vocabulary: The words used in a language, including their meanings and usage.

6. Communication: The exchange of information and ideas through spoken or written language.

7. Accent: The way in which a person pronounces words, often influenced by their regional or cultural background.

8. Active Listening: The process of fully concentrating, understanding, and responding to what another person is saying.

9. Constructive Feedback: Feedback that is given in a positive and helpful manner, with the goal of improving the recipient's performance or behavior.

10. Academic Writing: Formal writing done in an academic setting, often involving research and the use of scholarly sources.

11. Plagiarism: The act of using someone else's work or ideas without giving proper credit or attribution.

12. Cultural Sensitivity: The awareness and understanding of different cultural practices, beliefs, and values, and the ability to communicate and interact respectfully with individuals from different cultures.

13. Professionalism: The level of skill, competence, and behavior expected of a person in a professional setting.

Supporting Materials

Introduction:

- Crystal, D. (2003). English as a global language (2nd ed.). Cambridge University Press.

Chapter 1:

- Guffey, M. E., & Loewy, D. (2013). Business communication: Process and product (8th ed.). South-Western, Cengage Learning.

- Locker, K. O., & Kaczmarek, S. K. (2010). Business communication: Building critical skills (4th ed.). McGraw-Hill.

Chapter 2:

- Duarte, N. (2008). Slide:ology: The art and science of creating great presentations. O'Reilly Media.

- Reynolds, G. (2012). Presentation zen: Simple ideas on presentation design and delivery (2nd ed.). New Riders.

Chapter 3:

- Gerson, S. J., & Gerson, S. M. (2012). Technical writing: Process and product (6th ed.). Pearson Education.

- Weiss, E. (2013). How to write reports and proposals (3rd ed.). Barron's Educational Series.

Chapter 4:

- Fine, H. (2010). The etiquette edge: Modern manners for business success. AMACOM.

- Martin, J. N., & Nakayama, T. K. (2010). Experiencing intercultural communication: An introduction (4th ed.). McGraw-Hill.
Chapter 5:
- Hargie, O., & Tourish, D. (2009). Auditing organizational communication: A handbook of research, theory and practice. Routledge.
- O'Rourke, J. S., & Bowie, N. E. (2013). The ethics of workplace privacy. John Wiley & Sons.
Chapter 6:
- Brewer, E., & Gaskill, P. (2016). Exploring idiomatic creativity in beginner English textbooks. TESOL Quarterly, 50(2), 368-382.
- Proverbidioms. (1995). T. Denny & R. M. Licko (Eds.). Running Press.
Chapter 7:
- Hacker, D. (2011). A writer's reference (7th ed.). Bedford/St. Martin's.
- Turabian, K. L., Booth, W. C., Colomb, G. G., Williams, J. M., & Bizup, J. (2013). A manual for writers of research papers, theses, and dissertations: Chicago style for students and researchers (8th ed.). University of Chicago Press.
Conclusion:

- Carnegie, D. (2010). How to win friends and influence people (Special Anniversary Edition). Simon & Schuster.
- Pink, D. H. (2011). Drive: The surprising truth about what motivates us. Riverhead Books.

www.ingramcontent.com/pod-product-compliance
Lightning Source LLC
LaVergne TN
LVHW011032200726
843509LV00011B/1254